Unnegotiated Self

Building a Life from Alignment, not Survival

Felicia Mycyk

Amplify the Leader Within

Library of Congress Control Number: 2026900535

For information regarding special discounts for bulk purchases, speaking engagements, workshops, or facilitated discussions related to this book, visit **AmplifyTheLeaderWithin.com**.

Book Cover by Yasir Nadeem

Illustrations by Breyanne Mycyk

First edition 2025

COPYRIGHTS

ISBN 979-8-218-89727-7 (paperback)
ISBN 979-8-218-89833-5 (ebook)

Contents

To my mother,
whose creativity, entrepreneurship, and way with people
taught me how perception becomes expression

To my children,
your life is yours to design
the narrative is shaped by how you see
and how you choose to express

To my brothers, nieces, and nephews,
we creatively learned to love,
then we learned what was missing,
so now we choose how we connect

**To friends, extended family, and those who chose
me,**
we choose effort over ease,
presence across distance,
to be in connection

Love you.

Foreword

Written by Erin Ninehouser

To call Felicia Mycyk a gift to those around her is to stretch the limits of the word's definition. There is a fire deep within her that lights up every single project and person she's touched through her work as a community-builder, storyteller, coach, author, and educator.

Whether it's helping a young athlete find their power, understanding the pain of a nurse or teacher on the edge of burnout, or having the vision to invite people connected by proximity to relate as neighbors, Felicia instinctively knows how to create the transformation we desire because she's lived it herself.

She listens deeply, observes carefully, teaches wisely, and challenges fearlessly to help those around her remember, or perhaps for the first time, to discover their Unnegotiated Self. That clarity provides the spark that lights one's path to emotional healing, freedom, and joy.

Readers of this book will not only find a friend and fellow traveler in Felicia, but the strength and permission to create a life that honors and celebrates who they truly are.

About the Foreword Author:

Erin Ninehouser is a documentary photographer and storyteller whose work centers on the question, "What does it look like to care?" for your people, your purpose, and your community. Her artistic vision is informed by nearly two decades of nonprofit experience in advocacy and community organizing, and a deep desire to elevate the common good and inspire others to create a world where all people are valued.

Opening Note

The moment before the decision

I lost everything.

I lost my health.
I lost the version of family I thought would hold.
At one point, it felt like I lost my life.

What I didn't see at first was how isolated I had become.
The people around me weren't unkind, but no one interrupted. No one stepped in. No one said, "Here's what you need. Here's the next step."

Eventually, I understood.
No one was coming to save me.

I wrote down the names of every person I had shared something personal with. Vulnerability never came easily to me. When I looked at that list, I saw it clearly.

I stopped asking.
I stopped explaining.

I stopped waiting for someone else to name what I already knew.

I was the plan.

So I sat with that.

I decided to stop reliving the hurt.

That's when I connected with God. Not for answers, but for grounding. For stillness. For the strength to stay.

I had reached the last place.
And the last place meant choice.

So I started listening to the same words I had spent years offering everyone else.

When I chose peace, everything around me reacted.

But something had shifted.

I started listening to myself.

This book was written from that quiet place.
Not from urgency.
Not from reaction.
Not from needing to prove or explain anything.

I've spent years coaching others, stepping in, offering clarity, helping people move when they feel stuck. That work has always mattered to me.

But this season required something different.

I had to stop looking outward and stay with myself, not because I didn't know the work, but because this moment demanded that I live it without distraction.

Every reflection in these pages comes from my lived experience, shaped with intention and clarity.

I learned that progress doesn't come from force.
It comes from pausing long enough to choose with clarity.

The questions that follow each chapter are not prompts for fixing yourself.

They are pauses that reflect how leadership begins, with awareness, choice, and restraint.

What you're holding isn't a guide to fix yourself.

It's an invitation to lead yourself with awareness, intention, and trust.

You don't need permission to choose peace.
You don't need agreement to set boundaries.
You don't need certainty to move forward.

You only need to D.E.C.I.D.E.
This is where it begins.

PART ONE: SETTLING

"Clarity begins when the noise stops."

- COACH FELICIA MYCYK

Chapter 1
Now I choose peace without explaining myself
(Foundation, Boundary, Emotional Safety)

Chapter 2
Now I lead from clarity, not urgency
(Intentional Action, Mindful Pace)

Chapter 3
Now I trust my timing
(Self-Trust, Releasing Pressure)

Clarity begins when the noise stops.

PART I: SETTLING

Chapter 1

Now I choose peace without explaining myself

(Foundation, boundary, emotional safety)

Peace, to me, sounds like quiet.

My mind isn't scattered. There's space. I have time to think, time to decide, time to choose.

I'm not rushed. I'm not anxious to fill space with people or noise or urgency. I know who I want to be around. I know where I want to be. And I'm not afraid of the pauses in between.

I listen more now. Not to respond, not to react, just to listen.

Peace feels relaxed. I go to work and I'm okay with what I'm working on. I'm okay with who I'm going to see. It's not excitement I'm chasing, it's steadiness.

I can hear someone without feeling emotionally hijacked. I'm not scared. I'm not anxious. There's no static in the background.

And when distractions show up, peace looks like handling them without losing myself.

Peace feels easy. It feels comforting. It feels familiar.

I'm not forcing connection. I'm not reacting to everything around me. I'm not trying to be understood.

I'm just here.

Curious. Present. Open.

Peace, I've learned, feels like curiosity. It allows room for thought instead of fear.

All of this together feels normal. And I think this is what normal was always meant to feel like.

When sadness shows up now, I recognize it. I understand where it comes from. It moves through without taking over.

That's peace to me. Not the absence of emotion, but the presence of clarity.

Pause

Where in my life am I still explaining choices
that are already clear to me?

Chapter 2

Now I lead from clarity, not urgency

(How peace changes leadership and decisions)

Clarity guides the way I lead by slowing me down.

I take time. I listen. I lead to understand.

When I show up with people now, curiosity comes first. I want to understand what's actually happening, not what I assume is happening.

I've learned that the power is in the question. Not the answer. Not the fix.

So I don't rush conversations anymore. I'm not trying to move people along. I'm trying to see what's really there.

Sometimes I still feel the pull to move quickly. I notice it. And I check myself.

Because I'm not here to rescue anyone. And I don't want to react from instinct instead of insight.

Clarity means I pause long enough to respond well.

I want to be the best version of myself for the person in front of me, and that only happens when I'm not overreacting or overstepping. Taking my time allows me to understand what's happening and see clearly.

I like seeing things from multiple angles. I listen from different viewpoints. I consider what I'm hearing, what I'm observing, and what I'm feeling.

Then ground myself in my own perspective because I'm responsible for how I show up, not for controlling how others receive it.

I don't assume I know how something feels for someone else. I ask. Because I can't understand another person's experience without giving them space to share it.

Clarity requires listening beyond words.

I pay attention to body language. To tone. To emotion. To what's happening around the conversation, not just inside it.

I ask better questions now. And I wait for real answers.

Before I make decisions, I make sure I understand. Before I respond, I make sure I'm clear.

That's how I lead now. Not fast. Not reactive. Not urgent.

Clear. Curious. Intentional.

Pause

What feels urgent right now, and what feels truly important?

Chapter 3

Now I trust my timing

(Releasing pressure, comparison, and rushing)

Trusting my timing means I do my part, and then I let go.

I show up. I follow through. I do what I'm supposed to do.

And then I move on with my life.

I don't rush outcomes anymore. I don't chase answers. I don't need immediate confirmation that something is meant for me.

If it's right, it will open. If it's not, it won't.

Either way, I'm okay.

I've learned that timing isn't passive. It's intentional.

I do the work that's mine to do, and I stop there.
I don't replay conversations.
I don't reread messages.
I don't sit in anticipation or anxiety.

Timing isn't about waiting for something to happen. It's about planting what you want to grow and trusting the season to do its work.

I reap what I sow now, because I'm mindful of what I put into the ground.

I wait without waiting.

Trusting my timing means I don't try to skip steps. I let things unfold in the order they're meant to unfold.

I don't force doors. I don't pry them back open. I don't take rejection personally.

When a door opens, I walk through it. When a door closes, I accept it.

Not with frustration, but with understanding.

I trust that what's meant for me will recognize me. I know what I bring to the table now. I don't need to prove it or convince anyone of it.

If it fits, it stays. If it doesn't, I move.

And I don't compare my path to anyone else's.

Trusting my timing has made my life calmer. More relaxed. More grounded.

When something is right, I feel it. And when something ends, I don't panic.

I see closed doors as information, not failure. Sometimes they're protection. Sometimes they're redirection.

Either way, I keep moving.

That's what trusting my timing looks like now. Doing my part. Letting go. And knowing that what's meant for me will arrive when it's time.

Pause

---◄◆►---

What would I stop forcing if I trusted my timing completely?

PART TWO: CHOOSING

"What you allow becomes what you live with."

- COACH FELICIA MYCYK

Chapter 4
Now I stop before I overgive
(Energy Management, Setting Limits)

Chapter 5
Now I listen to my body and believe it
(Embodiment, Inner Wisdom)

Chapter 6
Now I respond instead of react
(Emotional Regulation, Presence)

Chapter 7
Now I don't negotiate my values
(Integrity, Non-Compromise)

Chapter 8
Now I allow joy to be simple
(Simplicity, Finding Delight)

What you allow becomes what you live with.

Chapter 4

Now I stop before I overgive

(Energy, boundaries, self-respect)

I recognize my limits now because I pay attention.

I notice when I'm giving past the point of balance. When I'm sharing too much. When I'm stepping into roles I haven't been invited into.

I can feel when something shifts from generosity to overextension.

There's a moment now where I pause and ask myself, Is this aligned, or am I abandoning myself?

I've learned to notice when my time, energy, or expertise should be valued differently. When a conversation turns into unpaid labor. When a relationship hasn't earned the level of access I'm offering.

I no longer give just to be liked. I no longer give to fill space. And I no longer give to people who aren't ready to receive.

That was a hard pattern to unlearn.

For a long time, I believed saying yes was the answer to everything. Say yes and doors will open. Say yes and opportunities will come.

And while that can be true, I also learned something else.

Every yes costs something.

Now I know my capacity. And when I'm near full, I stop.

Because when I overgive, the things that matter most to me start to suffer. My focus. My energy. My joy.

My body tells me when it's too much. My mind knows before I admit it. And there's always a quiet signal that says, this needs a boundary.

I still give freely, but not blindly.

If I feel like there should be an exchange, that tells me something. Not that I'm wrong, but that the relationship may not be aligned.

I no longer confuse generosity with depletion.

Now I check in before I give more. I ask questions. I set expectations.

I let people know what I normally do, what my role is, and what comes next. Not to withhold, but to be clear.

Clarity protects both sides.

And here's what changed everything: I stopped over giving when I started caring for myself first.

Once I did that, everything else adjusted naturally.

I still show up. I still support. I still care.

I just don't abandon myself in the process.

That's what healthy giving looks like now.

Pause

Where does my giving turn into depletion instead of contribution?

Chapter 5

Now I listen to my body and believe it

(Self-trust, intuition, regulation)

My body tells me the truth.

And now, I believe it.

I used to override signals. I used to minimize them. I used to explain them away.

But over time, I became more aware. Not fearful, just aware.

Now I honor what my body is telling me, and I respond with respect.

If I'm tired, I rest. If I need a break, I take a break. I don't negotiate when my body asks.

I've also learned the difference between what my body needs and what my mind is carrying.

If I'm feeling emotion, I journal. If I'm holding tension, I move. If I feel stress rising, I breathe and recenter.

I pay attention to the small signals now.

I've learned to listen to my body without debating it.

If my back hurts, I stand up and stretch. If I feel resistance, I pause. If something feels heavy in my system, I don't ignore it.

I've learned that everything is connected. When one piece is off, other pieces start to feel it too.

So I listen earlier.

Sometimes I literally take a mental note in the moment. I'm feeling something. And I don't rush past it.

I let myself experience it, name it, and move through it.

That's how I learn myself.

Because the next time that feeling shows up, I recognize it faster, and I respond differently.

Sometimes that response is simple. "I need a minute." "I need to step away." "I need to reset."

I've stopped arguing with my body.

Instead, I take an audit.

If I'm tired, I ask why. Is it from me, or from something outside of me?

If it's from me, I adjust. If it's from the world around me, I prepare and manage my expectations.

That's what honoring my body looks like now, preparation.

I know what supports me. More water. Less caffeine when I need steadiness. Rest before a big day. Movement that keeps me grounded.

I also know what doesn't support me.

I stop pretending I'm unaffected.

The goal isn't perfection.

The goal is awareness, and care.

Because when I listen to my body, I'm more prepared for life.

Things don't shock my system the way they used to. Noise doesn't automatically throw me off. Unexpected moments don't take me under.

Not because life is always calm, but because I'm supported from the inside.

That's what changed.

I don't wait until my body is yelling.

I listen when it whispers.

And I build my life in a way that lets me feel how I want to feel, steady, clear, and capable.

Pause

What has my body been telling me that I've been explaining away?

Chapter 6

Now I respond instead of react

(Emotional maturity, restraint, strength)

What helps me pause now is remembering that I don't always know what the other person is carrying.

And they don't always know where I'm coming from either.

So I slow myself down.

Before I react, I notice the first feeling. That initial surge. And I tell myself, take a second.

Pausing didn't come naturally to me. It was something I had to learn and practice.

As a child, we react. As an adult, we choose.

Now, my pause can look different depending on the moment.

Sometimes it's silence. Sometimes it's taking a breath. Sometimes it's saying nothing at all while I think.

Sometimes I repeat what the other person just said. Not to challenge it, but to give myself space to process. This is what I'm hearing you say.

Sometimes I say it out loud, I'm processing right now. Give me a second.

That pause gives me clarity. For myself. And for the person in front of me.

Responding instead of reacting has changed my relationships.

People feel heard. They feel understood. And I trust myself more in the moment.

I've learned that not everything requires an immediate response.

Sometimes people are processing out loud. Sometimes they're venting. Sometimes they're still figuring out what they mean.

If I jump in too fast, I might respond to the wrong thing.

When I let conversations develop, they often go somewhere better than I expected. Clearer. More honest. More complete.

Pausing allows me to hear what's really being said.

I also pause with myself.

When something feels personal, I ask, Why am I reacting this way?

I listen to my body. If my heart is racing, that's information. If something feels tight, that matters.

Instead of pushing through, I slow down and let the moment settle.

Responding doesn't mean suppressing emotion. It means allowing space between feeling and action.

That space is where clarity lives.

And that's how I show up now. Not rushed. Not reactive. But present, intentional, and grounded.

Pause

What changes when I give myself space before responding?

Chapter 7
Now I don't negotiate my values

(Identity, integrity, alignment)

The values that guide me now are simple, and they're firm.

I value my peace. I value understanding. I value clarity. And I value active listening.

Active listening matters to me because it's how people feel respected. It's hearing someone and reflecting it back. It's staying curious instead of reacting.

I don't mind differences. People can see the world completely differently than I do.

What matters is how they come into the conversation.

I value people who want to understand, not just be heard. People who are willing to meet in the middle and find common ground. People who are curious, not defensive.

I don't want to explain myself into acceptance anymore. I don't want to ask, Do you hear me? Do you understand me?

I want to be in spaces where understanding is already valued.

That's become non-negotiable.

If someone isn't willing to listen, I don't force the conversation. If someone isn't asking questions, I don't perform for them. And if someone enters a conversation already set on being right, I don't stay.

I watch when I'm being pulled in. I don't engage in arenas where I don't belong, especially ones where someone else makes the rules and expects me to play along.

That's a boundary I keep for myself.

I come into conversations with curiosity. And I can tell quickly whether the other person values me or not.

I no longer bend on respect. I no longer tolerate behavior that dismisses or diminishes me.

Alignment doesn't mean agreement. It means shared respect.

If the behavior toward me feels off, I pay attention. If it doesn't feel good, I don't rationalize it.

Life is too short to live outside my values.

Living by my values feels steady. It feels clean. It feels like integrity.

I don't question myself the way I used to.

Because at the end of the day, I'm the one who has to stand behind my decisions. I'm the one who has to live with them.

When I decide now, I ask myself one thing: Would I stand in front of someone and own this choice?

If the answer is yes, I move forward.

If I'm treated like an option, I don't stay. I value being chosen. And I choose myself the same way.

That's what became non-negotiable once I knew who I was.

Pause

What value am I tempted to soften in order to stay connected?

Chapter 8
Now I allow joy to be simple

(Ease, presence, unforced happiness)

Joy, for me now, is uncomplicated.

It's laughing because something is funny to me, not because anyone else says it should be. It's dancing without thinking about who's watching.

Joy is experience.

Listening. Noticing. Learning something new. Feeling something unfamiliar.

If I'm experiencing something, I'm happy.

I wake up and I'm grateful that I get to open my eyes. I let the sunlight in. I keep my curtains open. I like the way light fills the room.

Joy feels like gratitude.

It's noticing simple things and thinking, wow, this is happening. It's being present enough to enjoy them.

Seeing someone else succeed brings me joy. Watching someone apply something I shared and see it work brings me joy.

That's part of why I coach.

Whether it's an athlete adjusting their movement, a team finding its rhythm, or a leader stepping into clarity watching growth happen makes me happy.

I don't overthink it anymore. I don't analyze joy while it's happening.

I just enjoy life.

Joy feels like being here. Fully present. Nothing forced.

If something sounds fun, I'm in. If the music hits, I move. The genre doesn't matter.

I don't complicate happiness anymore. I don't complicate rest. I don't complicate contentment.

My energy has changed. My perspective has changed.

Perception is reality, and I get to choose mine.

I move through life at a pace that feels right to me.
I let myself enjoy what I enjoy.
I don't judge my joy against anyone else's.

I think about it the way I coached track.

I stopped measuring myself against anything outside of me.
It was never about beating the person next to you.
It was about being better than your last time.
Your last distance.
Your last effort.

What is my energy today? What perspective am I bringing into this moment?

When I stopped overthinking joy, everything became easier.

I became more present.

More relaxed.

More alive.

Because the only moment I can control is this one. Right now.

And right now is enough.

Pause

What kind of joy feels uncomplicated and honest to me right now?

PART THREE: BUILDING

"Alignment builds what urgency never
could"

- COACH FELICIA MYCYK

Chapter 9
Now I let life feel good
(Permission to Receive, Openness)

Chapter 10
Now I build from alignment, not survival
(Purpose, Deep Transformation)

Chapter 11
Now I honor who I am becoming
(Evolution, Future Self)

Alignment builds what urgency never could

UNNEGOTIATED SELF

Chapter 9

Now I let life feel good

(Receiving without guilt)

Receiving goodness now looks simple.

When someone gives me a compliment, I say thank you. I don't discount it. I don't explain it away. I don't shrink it.

I used to feel uncomfortable receiving. Awards, recognition, even kindness felt undeserved.

Now, I let it land.

If someone notices me, I allow that. If someone offers support, I accept it. If someone gives, I receive with gratitude.

I've stopped apologizing for what I've earned. I put the work in. I showed up. I took the time.

Even the simplest things matter.

I woke up today. I took care of myself. I showed up as I am.

That's worth acknowledging.

There was a time when small inconveniences could throw me off.
Remembering what it felt like not to have ease keeps me grounded.

That memory doesn't make me anxious, it makes me grateful.

Gratitude is how I receive goodness now.

I notice it. I name it. Sometimes I say it out loud. Sometimes I write it down.

Every morning, I give thanks for another day. Every night, I give thanks for making it through.

My prayers have changed.

I don't ask for everything to change. I ask for the strength to move through what is and the clarity to see what could be.

I let support exist around me.
I don't resist it.
I don't question it

Letting life feel good has shifted my energy.

I pay attention to how spaces feel. If something feels off, I don't force myself to stay. I trust that instinct and move accordingly.

I no longer brace for the other shoe to drop.

When something unexpected happens, I handle it. Not with panic, but with perspective.

Not everything is a crisis. Most things are just moments to navigate.

I start with the positive now. In conversations. In feedback. In how I see people.

If someone crosses my mind, I let them know. A message. A kind word. A moment of appreciation.

I don't wait for the perfect time to express gratitude.

Love moves best when it's genuine.

And I've learned to be honest with myself.

If I know I'm not going to show up as my best self, I pause. I rest. I take space.

That's part of letting life feel good too.

I know myself now.
I know when to lean in.
And I know when to step back.

I allow goodness without questioning it.

And presence has made life feel lighter and steadier.

Pause

Where am I resisting ease, even when it's available?

Chapter 10

Now I build from alignment, not survival

(Work, purpose, leadership, life design)

Building my life from alignment means I finally have space to choose.

For a long time, my life moved in a sequence. From school to responsibility. From role to role. From urgency to urgency.

There was very little pause. Very little room to ask what I actually wanted.

Survival required momentum. Alignment requires intention.

Now, I take time to think. I pay attention to what truly matters to me.

When you've lived in survival long enough, rebuilding teaches you quickly.

You know what pulls you backward.
You know what no longer fits.

I no longer stay where I have to brace.
I choose alignment over endurance.
I move forward without needing permission.

I don't build by default now. I build by alignment.

In work, relationships, and commitments I listen for fit. And when something feels off, I address it early.

If we're not aligned, I say it. Not with anger. Not with judgment.

Just clarity.

I no longer stay in situations hoping they will eventually feel right. I trust what I notice early.

Alignment doesn't mean I don't care. It means I care enough to be honest.

I no longer build my life around proving myself. I don't chase moving goalposts. And I don't give more just to create balance where it should already exist.

I don't mind growth. I don't mind benchmarks.

But when effort only benefits one side, that's not alignment.

I choose work that fits who I am. Even if it pays less. Even if it looks different.

I'd rather build something sustainable than sacrifice parts of myself for status or security.

Some people are motivated by money. That's their alignment.

Mine is purpose, people, and impact.

When something aligns, it doesn't feel like constant effort. It feels like an extension.

I've done work that drained me, and I've done work that energized me. I know the difference now.

I build from abundance, not scarcity.

I no longer believe this is the only opportunity, the only role, the only door. There will be others.

That belief alone changes how I choose.

I also pay attention to burnout.

If I feel overwhelmed, I pause. I speak it out loud. I adjust.

Burnout doesn't mean weakness. It means something is misaligned.

Alignment has given me stability. Clarity. Sustainability.

I can build for the long term now because I'm not forcing myself into roles that drain me.

When I do what aligns with who I am, I don't burn out. I expand.

Energy is a resource. And I manage it intentionally.

That's what building from alignment looks like now.

Thoughtful. Honest. Sustainable.

And for the first time, it feels like I'm building a life that actually fits me.

Pause

What would I build differently if survival were no longer the driver?

Chapter 11

Now I honor who I am becoming

(Growth without pressure)

I give myself permission to evolve now by not waiting for approval.

If I want to try something, I try it. If I want to learn something, I learn it. I don't need permission to change my life.

I think about it simply.

If you want to bake a cake, you don't enroll in a program and wait for a certificate. You decide to bake a cake. You find what you need. You try.

That's how I approach growth now.

I stopped believing someone else had to validate my readiness.

Instead, I lead myself with curiosity.

I've learned to be patient with myself. To allow grace. To treat myself the way I would treat someone I care about.

I no longer demand perfection. I no longer rush timelines. I no longer perform for progress.

I pay attention to my energy.

When I manage my energy well, I have space. And when unexpected things show up, they don't take over my life.

I don't need to be "on" all the time.

I've learned to step out of urgency and into what feels like my best life. A place where I get to choose. A place where decisions don't consume everything else.

Honoring my becoming means asking myself what actually supports me. And letting go of what doesn't.

If I see something I want, I don't compare myself. I don't rush. I don't judge where I am.

I make a plan.

I move at my own pace.

I don't want to become someone else. I want to become more of me.

And when I do what I said I would do, I let myself feel proud. I celebrate the small wins. Moment by moment. Day by day.

That's how I rewire my mind now.

If I get pushed back, I reset. And I keep going.

There's no single right path. There's just choosing what feels right, again and again.

When I stopped trying to arrive somewhere, everything changed.

I started enjoying the moment I was in. I stopped performing. I stopped proving.

I showed up as myself.

And I had more fun.

People responded differently. And more importantly, I liked myself more.

That's what honoring my becoming looks like now.

Not rushing. Not comparing. Just growing, steadily, into who I already am.

Pause

What version of myself am I learning to trust?

PART FOUR: LIVING

"Nothing is missing."

- COACH FELICIA MYCYK

Chapter 12
Now I live grounded, grateful, and present
(Integration, Daily Practice, Presence)

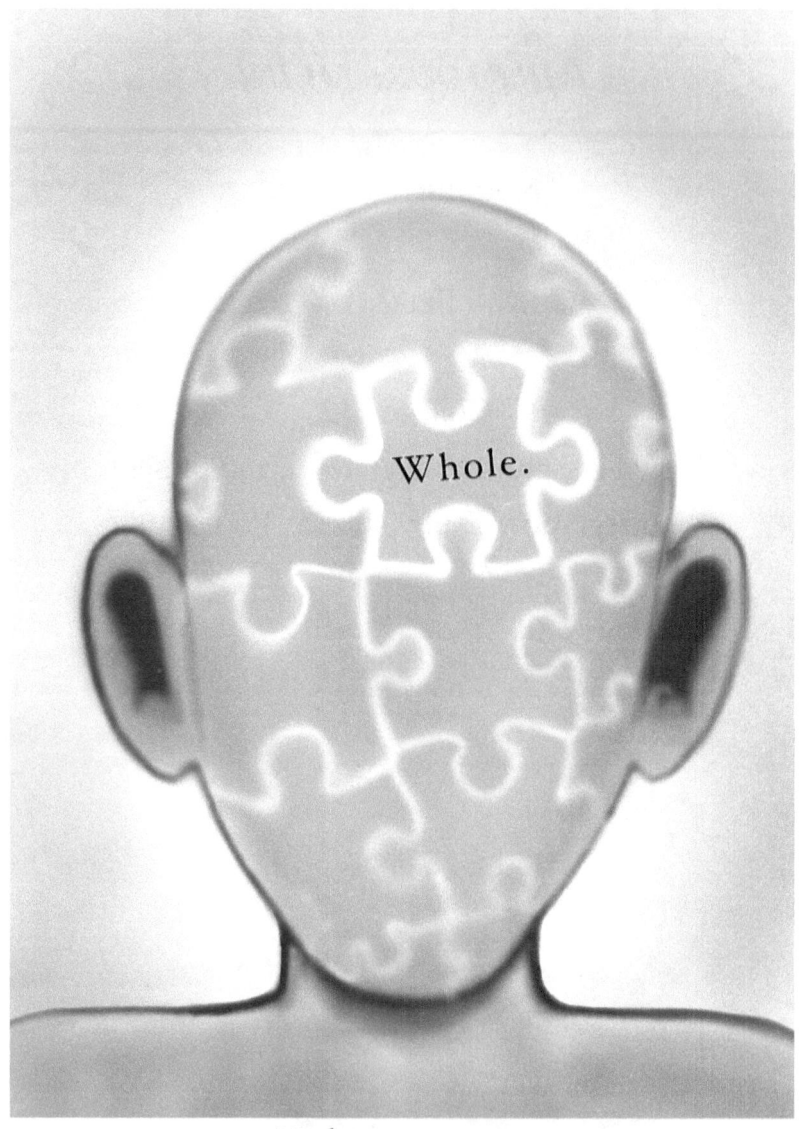

Nothing is missing.

PART IV: LIVING

Chapter 12

Now I live grounded, grateful, and present

(Integration)

Living fully in the present now feels steady.

I wake up grateful. I thank God for the day and for the chance to begin again.

At night, I give thanks for making it through the day. For the moments I noticed. For the ones I enjoyed.

I ask for others to be well. To rest. To wake up and try again tomorrow.

That rhythm keeps me grounded.

Each day, I think about my energy. How I'm using it. How I'm caring for it.

I ask myself one simple question: How can I be a little better than I was yesterday?

Not perfect. Just present.

I take pride in myself now. And when I do, I move through the world differently.

I lead with kindness. I try not to act from spite or pettiness. I stay aware.

Gratitude shows up in how I notice people. How I respect different perspectives. How I appreciate effort, including my own.

I don't feel the need to rush past moments anymore.

I believe we all move forward when we help one another. And that each generation can make life a little better for the next.

Living present has softened everything.

Nothing feels as devastating as it once did. I still feel emotion. I still experience intensity.

But I know how to ground myself again.

I know when to step back. I know which conversations to avoid. I know how to return to calm.

I live in a quieter, more peaceful place now.

An ordinary good day feels like laughter.
Like dancing.
Like being glad to see someone.

It feels like smiling because it's genuine.

I'm comfortable with others. And I'm comfortable with myself.

I no longer confuse solitude with isolation.

Now, solitude is a choice. A reset. A way to listen to myself again.

I can spend hours alone and feel full. And I can be around people and feel connected.

I know what I need.

And I allow myself to enjoy it.

A good nap. A simple plan. A moment of rest.

That's what a good life feels like now.

Grounded. Grateful. Present.

And that's where I live.

Pause

What does being present look like in my ordinary, everyday life?

Where This Continues

This book was written in a season where I stopped explaining and started choosing with clarity.

Over time, I realized this work wasn't meant to stay on the page alone. The reflections, decisions, and pause moments you've encountered here are the same principles I facilitate with leaders, teams, and organizations who are ready to lead without urgency, burnout, or self-abandonment.

If this book resonated with you, you don't have to carry the work forward on your own. You're invited to continue it through facilitated conversation, leadership development, or guided reflection.

To support that next step, you can download facilitation discussion prompts designed to help individuals and groups slow down, reflect, and apply this work in real time.

Wherever this work meets you next, trust that clarity will continue to guide what comes next.

Speaking, Workshops & Facilitation Resources

www.AmplifyTheLeaderWithin.com

About the author

Felicia Mycyk is an award-winning leadership development speaker and coach, and a mother, who helps people move out of survival mode and into lives led by clarity, peace, and intentional choice.

Her work lives at the intersection of story and leadership, grounded in the belief that growth is cultivated, not rushed, and that meaningful change comes in its proper season. Transformation requires patience, consistency, and care. Felicia's coaching is shaped by lived experience, seasons of loss and healing, and the daily practice of leading with presence, both personally and professionally.

She is the creator of the D.E.C.I.D.E. Self-Leadership© framework, a practical model for self-awareness, resilience, and aligned decision-making. Through speaking, workshops, and coaching, Felicia walks alongside individuals and leaders as they do the inner work that leads to sustainable growth, not burnout or performance alone.

Drawing on fundamental sport coaching principles, Felicia Mycyk helps individuals, young people, entrepreneurs, and teams develop self-leadership, strengthening their ability to lead themselves before leading others. Her approach emphasizes discipline, awareness, consistency, and trust in the process, skills that translate far beyond the field.

At the heart of her message is a gentle faith, one that trusts that while we plant and water, growth ultimately comes from something greater than ourselves. We are created with intention, shaped over time, and meant to bear fruit in season.

Felicia lives in Pennsylvania and continues to create spaces where people feel safe to grow, grounded enough to wait, and confident enough to choose alignment over urgency.

www.FeliciaMycyk.com